DATE DUE NOV 1 1 1992

91

91

32

192

What?

A

Riddle
Book

WHAT? a Riddle book

By Jane Sarnoff and Reynold Ruffins

Technical consultant
SIMMS TABACK

Printed in the United States of America/Library of Congress Catalog Card Number 74-9592/ISBN 0-684-13911-1
3 5 7 9 11 13 15 17 19 RD/C 20 18 16 14 12 10 8 6 4 2

Charles Scribner's Sons
New York

To Barbara, Ben,

Beth, Bradley, Dafna, Daniel,

Daniella, Eric, John, Lise, Lynn, Seth, and Todd

Grung, groop, grakity, gree

Children make something that no one can see.

What is it?

NOISE.

Why does time fly so fast?
Because so many people are trying to kill it.

When can you see through a friend?
When she has a pain in her stomach.

Two men dug a hole in five days. How many days did it take them to dig half a hole?
You can't dig half a hole.

What did the baby ghost say to the bully ghost?
Leave me alone or I'll tell my mummy.

When can you have an empty pocket and still have something in it?
When you have a hole in your pocket.

What should you do when you wear your pants out?
Wear them in again.

What kind of clothing lasts the longest?
Underwear. It is never worn out.

What's always behind time?
The back of a clock.

What is The Lone Ranger's first name?
The.

Why does a dog wag his tail?
Because no one else will wag it for him.

How many legs has a mule if you call a tail a leg?
Four. Even if you call a tail a leg it is still a tail.
(Abraham Lincoln)

What would you do if an elephant sat in front of you at the movies?
Miss most of the movie.

Which side of a hamburger is the left side?
The part that isn't eaten.

Why is a baker of hamburger rolls like a beggar?
Because he kneads the dough.

When did the Irish potato change nationality?
When it became French fried.

Mr. Hamburger is a butcher. He is 6'1" tall and wears a size 11 shoe. What does he weigh?
Meat.

What is it everyone would like to have yet wants to get rid of right away?
A good appetite.

How do you make a hamburger for an elephant?
First you get a big roll...

What do elephants eat besides hamburgers?
Canned elephant food.

What resembles half a hamburger?
The other half.

How many hamburgers can you eat on an empty stomach?
One. After that your stomach isn't empty.

How can five persons divide five hamburgers so that everyone gets one and one still is on the plate?
One person takes the plate with the hamburger.

If cheese comes on top of a hamburger, what comes after cheese?
A mouse.

A cook cooked two dozen hamburgers. All but eleven were eaten. How many were left?
Eleven.

What passes many hamburger stands without moving?
The highway.

What smells most at a hamburger stand?
The nose.

What did the cat say when it met the mouse?
Burp.

How can you catch a wild rabbit?
Make a noise like a carrot.

What is orange and half a mile high?
The Empire State Carrot.

What does the lamp post become when the lamp is removed?
A lamplighter.

What is the difference between here and there?
The letter T.

Why did the carpenter refuse to hit the nail with his hammer?
Because it was his thumbnail.

If a woman is born in Russia, grows up in Africa, moves to America, and dies in Pottstown, Pennsylvania, what is she?
Dead.

Why is the letter B like a fire?
Because it makes oil boil.

Why is an old car like a baby?
Because it always has a rattle.

What did the leopard say when it started to rain?
That hits the spots.

If all the people in a country owned pink cars, what would that country be called?
A pink car nation.

Why is Sunday the strongest day?
Because it isn't a weekday.

When is a door not a door?
When it is ajar.

Why is an unmarried man like a sharpshooter?
Because he never Mrs. anyone.

What is smaller than an ant's mouth?
An ant's dinner.

What time is it when an elephant sits on a fence?
Time to get a new fence.

W hat makes a fire-engine dog spotted?
His spots.

How do you know that cooks are mean?
Because they beat eggs and whip cream.

What is brought to the table and cut, but never eaten?
A deck of cards.

Why didn't the skeleton cross the road?
It didn't have the guts.

If a girl ate her mother and her father, what would that make her?
An orphan.

Why is summer like the letter N?
Because it makes ice nice.

Why is lettuce the most loving vegetable?
Because it is all heart.

How many big men have been born in California?
None. Only babies.

What comes once in a minute, once in a month, but never
in a hundred years?
The letter M.

Why is W the nastiest letter?
Because it always makes ill will.

What did one railroad car say to the other?
Let's get hitched.

If you breathe oxygen in the daytime, what do you breathe in the
nighttime?
Nitrogen.

What do you get when you cross a parrot with an elephant?
An animal that tells what it remembers.

Why was the baby raised on monkey milk?
Because it was a baby monkey.

What happens when a cat eats a lemon?
It becomes a sour puss.

What insect would make the best outfielder?
A spider. It always catches flies.

How do you stop a rooster from crowing early on Sunday morning?
Eat it Saturday night.

What is hard to beat?
A hard-boiled egg.

What is worse than a centipede with sore feet?
A giraffe with a sore throat.

Why does a cat, when it enters a room, look first to one side and then to the other?
Because it can't look to both sides at the same time.

When does a chimp chase a banana?
When the banana splits.

What animal eats with its tail?
They all do. None of them can remove their tails to eat.

Why isn't a dog's nose twelve inches long?
Because if it were it would be a foot.

What did the dog say to the flea?
Don't bug me.

What did one flea say to the other when they came out of the movies?
Shall we walk home or take a dog?

What do you get when you cross a canary and a tiger?
I don't know, but when it sings you'd better listen.

Why does a horse have six legs?
Because he has forelegs in the front and two in the back.

What insect goes skindiving?
A mosquito.

What did the boy octopus say to the girl octopus?
I want to hold your hand, hand, hand, hand, hand, hand, hand, hand.

What is the principal part of a horse?
The mane part.

What animal do you look like when you take a bath?
A little bear.

Which has more legs, a horse or no horse?
No horse. A horse has four legs but no horse has eight legs.

Why are alley cats like unskillful surgeons?
Because they mew till late and destroy patience.

What did the bad frog say to the good frog?
I hope you croak.

When did the apple turn over?
When it saw the jelly roll.

In what month do politicians talk the least?
February. It's the shortest month.

Every morning the farmer had eggs for breakfast. He owned no chickens and he never got eggs from anyone else's chickens. Where did he get the eggs?
From his ducks.

What will make pies sneaky?
The letter S will make spies of them.

What is the fastest way to double your dollars?
Fold them.

What is the difference between illegal and unlawful?
One is a sick bird and the other is against the law.

What is the difference between a dancer and a duck?
One goes quick on her beautiful legs and the other goes quack on her beautiful eggs.

Which hand do the English use to stir their tea?
Neither. They use a spoon.

What do you call a woman who doesn't have all her fingers on one hand?
Normal. Her fingers are divided between her two hands.

What do you take off last before you go to bed?
You take your feet off the floor.

If all the other animals went into the ark in pairs, why didn't the worms?
Because they went in apples.

Who is Tarzan's favorite folk singer?
Harry Elephanté.

What would a cannibal be who ate his mother's sister?
An aunt eater.

What is the difference between a deer running from its chasers and a midget witch?
One is a hunted stag and the other is a stunted hag.

Why are sidewalks in the winter like music?
Because if you don't C-sharp you will B-flat.

What is it that if you take away all the letters will remain the same?
A postperson.

What do people in England call little black cats?
Kittens.

How can plumbers tell what the weather will be without using weather instruments?
Listen to the weather forecast.

Why is the letter D dangerous?
Because it makes ma mad.

Why does your sense of touch suffer when you are ill?
Because you don't feel well.

What is it that has nothing left but a nose when it loses an eye?
The word noise.

Why was George Washington buried at Mt. Vernon?
Because he was dead.

How does a coffee pot feel when it's full?
Perky.

What must you do to the alphabet to remove A from it?
B-head it.

Why do so many elephants wear bright green nail polish?
So they can hide in the pea patch.

W hat did the penny say to the dime?
It would make more cents if we went together.

A farmer had 2½ haystacks in one row and 3½ haystacks in another row. How many haystacks did he have when he put them together?
One.

If two Texas telegraph operators were married, what would they become?
A Western Union.

Why are the Middle Ages called the Dark Ages?
Because there were so many knights.

What did the light switch say to the boy?
Boy, do you turn me on!

What letter would a deaf woman most like to have?
An H because it would make her ear hear.

Why was the little shoe so bad?
Its mother was a sneaker and its father was a loafer.

How can you make money fast?
Glue it down.

Why is a turkey like a ghost?
Because it's always a-gobblin'.

When should a baker stop making doughnuts?
When he gets tired of the hole business.

What gates are like church bells?
Toll gates.

Why did the man take hay to bed with him?
To feed his nightmares.

How can you trail an elephant in the jungle?
By the slight smell of peanuts on its breath.

What is the difference between a watchmaker and a prison warden?
One sells watches and the other watches cells.

When is a piece of wood like a king?
When it is a ruler.

What is a hole in the middle?
A ring.

Why is a wild horse like an egg?
Because it must be broken before it can be used.

Why can't vampires start a baseball game in the afternoon?
Because the bats don't come out until night.

When is coffee like the surface of the earth?
When it is ground.

What is never out of sight?
The letter S.

What kind of robbery is not dangerous?
A safe robbery.

What did one candle say to the other?
Are you going out tonight?

Why did the rooster refuse to fight?
Because it was chicken.

What did the cradle say to the baby?
Let's have a swinging time.

On the way to the water hole a zebra met 6 elephants. Each elephant had 3 monkeys on its head and each monkey had 2 birds on its tail. How many animals were going to the water hole?
Only the zebra. All the rest were going away from the water hole.

Which astronaut wears the largest helmet?

The one with the largest head.

Why did the moon go to the bank?

To change quarters.

Why is T the most powerful letter?

It can make a star start.

What is the astronaut's favorite meal?

Launch.

What holds the sun up?

Sun beams.

When the astronauts first landed on the moon, where did they stand?

On their feet.

18

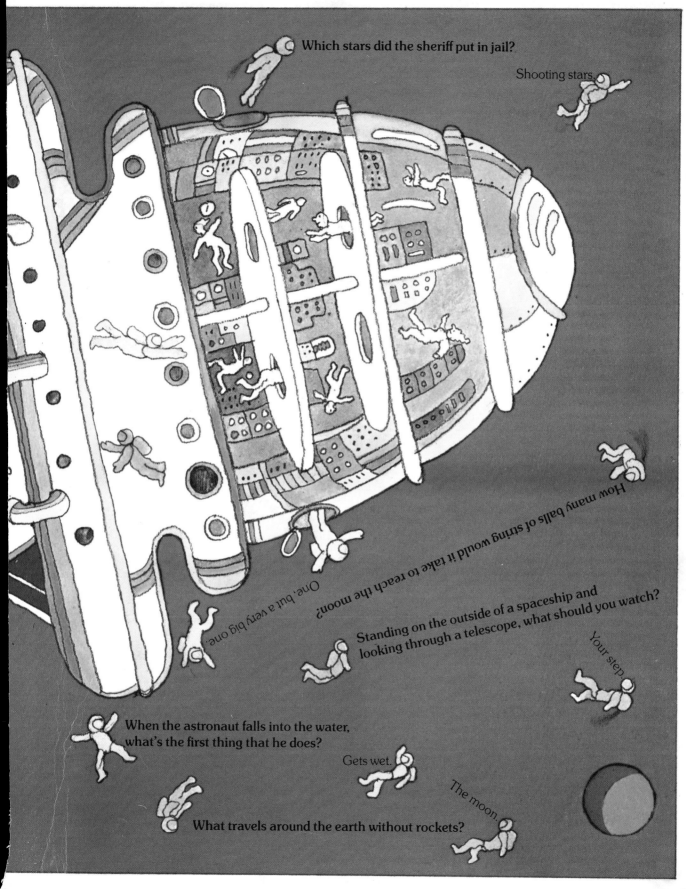

Which stars did the sheriff put in jail?

Shooting stars.

How many balls of string would it take to reach the moon?

One, but a very big one.

Standing on the outside of a spaceship and looking through a telescope, what should you watch?

Your step.

When the astronaut falls into the water, what's the first thing that he does?

Gets wet.

The moon.

What travels around the earth without rockets?

19

What can you keep when you give it away?
A cold.

If you can buy eight apples for twenty-six cents, how many can you buy for a cent and a quarter?
Eight.

Why should you never swim on an empty stomach?
It's easier to swim in water.

How do you make a lemon drop?
Just let it fall.

What's the best way to keep fresh cookies?
Don't return them.

When is a house not a house?
When it's afire.

How do you know that horses don't like oats?
They always say neigh to them.

What did one eye say to the other eye?
Just between us, something smells.

What is dark but made by light?
A shadow.

Why did the liar keep his word?
No one would take it.

What did the salad say to the spoon and fork?
You get me all mixed up.

Why does Santa have a garden?
Because he likes to go hoe, hoe, hoe.

Which is the west side of a little boy's pants?
The side the sun sets on.

What do you get when you cross an octopus with a pile of hay?
Eight straw brooms.

Who was the best runner in the Bible?
Adam. He was first in the human race.

How did Adam and Eve feel when they left the Garden of Eden?
Put out.

Where is tennis mentioned in the Bible?
Where Joseph served in Pharaoh's court.

Who was the busiest doctor in the Bible?
Job. He had the most patience.

When is medicine first mentioned in the Bible?
When God gave Moses two tablets.

Besides Adam, who in the Bible had no father?
Joshua. He was the son of Nun.

Who was the best actor in the Bible?
Samson. He brought the house down.

What fur did Adam and Eve wear?
Bareskin.

Who was the straightest man in the Bible?
Joseph. Pharaoh made a ruler of him.

Where is a walking stick mentioned in the Bible?
Where Eve presented Adam with a little Cain.

What did Eve do when she wanted sugar?
She raised Cain.

What was it that Adam never saw, never had, and still gave two of to his children?
Parents.

At what time of day was Adam created?
Just a little before Eve.

22

What bolt is never on a door? A thunderbolt.

What kind of paper should be used to make a kite?

Flypaper.

Where does Sunday come before Thursday? In the dictionary

Why is a March weather forecast like a baby?

Because it's always being changed.

Who shoots people, blows them up, and lets them go home and hang themselves? A photographer.

What is everyone in the world doing at the same time? Getting older.

23

When do boats become very affectionate?
When they hug the shore.

Why didn't Mother let the doctor operate on Father?
She didn't want anyone else to open her male.

What do you break by naming it?
Silence.

Why does a giraffe need so little to eat?
Because it makes a little go a long way.

What is a history of cars called?
An autobiography.

When does a caterpillar improve in behavior?
When it turns over a new leaf.

What part of London is in France?
The letter N.

What is the difference between a tailor and a stable boy?
One mends a tear and the other tends a mare.

What should a prize fighter drink?
Punch.

What is lower with a head than without it?
A pillow.

When is the letter Z not used in Japan?
When Japan is spelled right.

What is a store detective called?
A counter spy.

What is the best way to talk to a monster?
Long distance.

What do you do when an elephant sneezes?
Get out of the way.

What are the five animals in the giraffe family?
The mother giraffe, the father giraffe, and the three baby giraffes.

What has no feet but always wears shoes out?
The sidewalk.

How do you spell dried grass in three letters?
Hay.

What always has one eye open but cannot see?
A needle.

Where were potatoes first found?
In the ground.

What is the difference between a farmer and an actor?
One minds his peas and the other his cues.

What does a leopard become after it is five years old?
Six years old.

What two animals go everywhere you go?
Your calves.

How did the sailor know there wasn't a man in the moon?
He'd been to sea.

Where is Minute Street?
Between Sixty-first and Sixty-third streets.

Why did the butcher put bells on his scale?
Because he wanted to jingle all the weigh.

What did the tie say to the hat?
Don't just hang around, go on ahead.

Why is a calendar sad?
Because its days are numbered.

How do you get down off an elephant?
You don't get down off an elephant, you get down off a duck.

Why did the busy bee call the flowers lazy?
Because they were always in bed.

What are the little rivers called that run into the Nile?
The juveniles.

What can fall into a well without rippling the water?
The sunshine.

When is a gardener like a mystery writer?
When he digs up a plot.

Why did Silly Sammy put bug spray on his watch?
Because it had ticks.

After the rain falls, when does it rise again?
In dew time.

How can you tell a dogwood tree from a pine tree?
By its bark.

What do you call a sleeping bull? A bulldozer.

Where does
a lamb go when it needs a haircut?

To the Baa Baa Shop.

What did the big flower
say to the little flower?
Hi, Bud.

Why does a watermelon
have so much water in it?
Because it is planted in the spring.

What do
bees do to earn
a living?

They cell their honey.

What is bought by the yard and worn by the foot?
A carpet.

What tree is the oldest?
The elder.

Why is a horseback rider like a cloud?
Because they both hold the reins.

What is a frightened skindiver called?
Chicken of the sea.

What is visible only in the winter?
Your breath.

What is most useful when it is used up?
An umbrella.

What has four legs, a back and two arms but no body?
A chair.

If April showers bring May flowers, what do May flowers bring?
Pilgrims.

Where does a witch keep her space ship?
In her broom closet.

Why aren't brides allowed to wear their trains any longer?
Because they are long enough.

What did one sandwich say to the other?
You're full of bologna.

What did the moon say to the star?
Boy, are you far out.

What is the most important use for cowhide?
To hold the cow together.

How can an elephant get to the top of a tree?
Sit on an acorn and wait.

The faster you run the harder I am to catch. What am I?
Your breath.

The greater it is, the less it can be seen. What is it?
Darkness.

I never ask questions, but I get many answers. What am I?
A doorbell.

No man wants me, but once he's got me, no man wants
to lose me. What am I?
A bald head.

The more you take away from it the bigger it becomes.
What is it?
A hole.

The more it gets, the more it eats, but when it has eaten
everything, it must die. What is it?
Fire.

Use me well and I am everybody. Scratch my back and
I am nobody. What am I?
A mirror.

I danced all night at a ball, but I am nothing at all. What am I?
A shadow.

The more it dries, the wetter it gets. What is it?
A towel.

As big as a house but lighter than a feather. What is it?
The shadow of a house.

Everyone can divide it, but no one can see the division.
What is it?
Water.

What word can be pronounced faster by adding another syllable to it?

Fast.

Why don't station wagons have to pay tolls at bridges?

Because their drivers pay them.

Where can you find roads without cars, forests without trees, and cities without houses?

On a map.

What is yellow and lies on its back?
A tired school bus.

What is the difference between a bus driver and a bad cold?
One knows the stops and the other stops the nose.

What did Paul Revere say when he finished his ride? Whoa.

What is a Camelot?
A place where they sell used camels.

How does a car go that has a horn, three wheels, and no engine? BEEP, BEEP.

Why can't a bicycle stand by itself? Because it's two tired.

When is a car not a car? When it is turning into a driveway.

Why do narrow roads like the letter B? It will make them broad.

What did the elephant say to the maharajah?

Get off my back.

Where do old Volkswagens go?

To the old Volks' home.

What is it that everyone, no matter how careful, overlooks?
A nose.

Why does the ocean roar?
Because it has crabs in its bed.

If an athlete gets athlete's foot, what does an astronaut get?
Missile toe.

What snake is good at math?
An adder.

What has many eyes but never cries?
A potato.

What has a thousand teeth and no mouth?
A saw.

What did the ocean say when the plane flew over?
Nothing. It just waved.

When was the shark shocked?
When it met the electric eel.

How can you fall off a fifty-foot ladder and not get hurt?
Fall off the bottom rung.

Why is an old chair as good as new when it has been lost and then found?
Because it has been re-covered.

What is the difference between a crazy rabbit and a counterfeit quarter?
One is a mad bunny and the other is bad money.

Why did the greenhouse call the doctor?
It had window pains.

How does an elephant get down from a tree?
Sits on a leaf and waits for fall.

Why is a nose in the middle of a face?
Because it is a scenter.

Why is it rude to whisper?
Because it is not aloud.

When is a black dog not a black dog?
When it is a greyhound.

Which is heavier, a half moon or a full moon?
A half moon, because a full moon is lighter.

What happens to the boy who misses his school bus?
He catches it when he gets home.

What is the difference between a 16-ounce baby and
a boy driving spikes into the ground?
One weighs a pound and the other pounds away.

If you were locked in a room with nothing but a baseball
bat, how would you get out?
Take three strikes.

Why do white sheep eat more than black sheep?
Because there are more of them.

Is there a word in the English language that contains
all the vowels?
Unquestionably.

Which is better, the house burned down or the
house burned up?
Neither. Both are very bad.

What is the difference between a fisherman and a lazy student?
One baits his hook and the other hates his book.

What is purple and 5,000 miles long?
The Grape Wall of China.

What are six ducks in a crate?
A box of quackers.

**What do you get when you
cross a duck with a cow?**
Milk and quackers.

**What geometric figure
is like a lost parrot?**

A polygon.

What bird is at every meal?
A swallow.

What is a crowbar?
A place where crows go to drink.

What bird can lift
the heaviest weight?
A crane.

What kind of
doctor would
a duck become?
A quack doctor.

What does a stork do
when it stands on
one foot?
It lifts up the other.

What did one owl
say to the other?
I don't give a hoot
about you.

What did the little chick say
when it found an orange in its nest?
Look at the orange Mama laid.

Why did the eagle fly over the mountain?
Because it couldn't fly under it.

Ruffins

What is the difference between a school teacher and a railroad conductor?
One trains the mind and the other minds the train.

What did the envelope say when it was licked?
It shut up and said nothing.

What's better than a horse that can count?
A spelling bee.

Who earns a living without doing a day's work?
A night watchman.

Why is your hand like a hardware store?
Because it has nails.

Where can you always find sympathy?
In the dictionary.

What did the witch say to the baby ghost?
Fasten your sheet belt.

What is always coming but never arrives?
Tomorrow.

Which is the rudest bird?
The mockingbird.

What is it that we often return but never borrow?
Thanks.

What did the porcupine say to the cactus?
Mama?

What did the kitten say to the tiger?
Peace, brother.

What kind of dress do you have but never wear?
Your address.

Where do baby elephants come from?
BIG storks.

Why do you forget a tooth after it is pulled?
Because it has gone right out of your head.

What has a neck but no head?
A bottle.

Why is it hard for a leopard to hide?
Because it is always spotted.

How did little Bo Peep lose her sheep?
She had a crook with her.

What is full of holes and holds water?
A sponge.

Why is a book like a king?
Because they both have pages.

What do you lose every time you stand up?
Your lap.

What did the ground say to the rain?
If you keep that up my name will be mud.

If your uncle's sister is not your aunt, how is she related to you?
She's your mother.

Why are fishermen so stingy?
Because their job makes them sell fish.

What's the best way to paint a rabbit?
With hare spray.

What is a witch's favorite plant?
Poison ivy.

Why did the bird fly south?
It was too far to walk.

How do you make an elephant float?
Two scoops of ice cream, some root beer, and an elephant.

Why did Silly Sammy stand in back of the mule?
He thought he'd get a kick out of it.

Why did Silly Sally throw tomato and lettuce around the room?
She wanted a tossed salad.

Why did Silly Sammy push his bicycle down the street?
He was late for an appointment and didn't have time to get on.

What did Silly Sally do with the leftover holes from doughnuts?
She tied them up with string to make fishnets.

Why did Silly Sally tell jokes to the mirror?
She liked to see it crack up.

Why did Silly Sammy's mother go out in the rain with her purse open?
She expected some change in the weather.

What did Silly Sammy say when he saw milk bottles in the grass?
Hey, look at the cow's nest.

Why did Silly Sally feed the cow money?
So she could get rich milk.

What did one of Silly Sammy's ears say to the other?
Do you live on this block too?

Why did Silly Sammy wear loud socks?
To keep his feet from falling asleep.

Why did Silly Sally take a ruler to bed with her?
To see how long she slept.

Why did Silly Sammy sit in front of the television set with milk and sugar?
He heard there was going to be a serial.

Why did Silly Sally go for a walk in the city with a piece of bread and butter?
She was looking for the traffic jam.

Why doesn't Silly Sammy use toothpaste?
None of his teeth are loose.

What did Silly Sally do when she thought she was dying?
She went into the living room.

Why did Silly Sammy put his father in the refrigerator?
He wanted cold pop.

Why did Silly Sally cut her fingers off?
She wanted to write shorthand.

Why did Silly Sammy sleep on the lamp?
He was a light sleeper.

Why did Silly Sally sit on the roof?
She heard that the treats were on the house.

What do you call elephants who ride on ocean liners?

Passengers.

What do you get when you cross a math teacher with a crab?

Snappy answers.

When is a sailor not a sailor?

When he's afloat.

Why can't you play cards on a small boat?

Because someone is always sitting on the deck.

When is a ship like a pile of snow?

When it's adrift.

How can you spell "hard water" in three letters?

Ice.

A box is filled with water and weighs a ton. What can you put in the box to make it weigh less?

Holes.

What would you drink if you were locked in a room with only a bed?

Water from the bed springs.

Why is a river richer than a vine?

Because a river has two banks, and a vine can't even support itself.

How do sailors get their clothes clean?

They throw them overboard and they are washed ashore.

dog

chase the catfis

What letters are never tired?
N,R,G.

What sheet can't be folded?
A sheet of ice.

Why is snow like a tree?
Because it leaves in the spring.

What should you do if you split your sides laughing?
Run until you get a stitch in them.

Why is a 9 like a peacock?
Because it's nothing without a tail.

What coat has no buttons and is put on wet?
A coat of paint.

Why can't a train sit down?
Because it has a tender behind.

Why is a lion in the desert like Christmas?
Because of its sandy claws.

Can you drive a car over water?
Sure. Just use the bridge.

What did the big firecracker say to the little firecracker?
My pop is bigger than your pop.

What did the canary say when its cage broke?
Cheep! Cheep!

How did the firefly feel when it ran into a fan?
Delighted.

Who can raise things without lifting them?
A farmer.

Why did the elephant sit on the marshmallow?
To keep from falling into the hot chocolate.

What is better than presence of mind in an automobile accident?
Absence of body.

Why is a rabbit's nose always shiny?
Because its powder puff is on the wrong end.

Why should a stupid kid study the letter P before taking a test?
Because it can make an ass pass.

Why is the job of President like a back tooth?
Because it is hard to fill well.

How do batteries get sick?
They get acid indigestion.

Why does a hen lay eggs?
Because if she dropped them they would break.

Why are birds such big eaters?
Because they take a peck at a time.

How can a shy child become a stone?
By becoming a little bolder.

When are you most like an automobile wheel?
At night when you are tired.

What is the longest word in the English language?
Smiles. There is a mile between the beginning and the end of it.

What did the sock say to the foot?
You're putting me on.

Why should you do your arithmetic lessons with a pencil?
Because the pencil can't do them without you.

How do you fit six elephants in a Volkswagen?
Three in the front seat and three in the back.

*Why was
the little strawberry worried?*

His mom and dad
were in a jam.

*What kind of nut
has some of its inside
outside?*

A doughnut.

*What's the best way
to catch a squirrel?*

Climb a tree and act
like a nut.

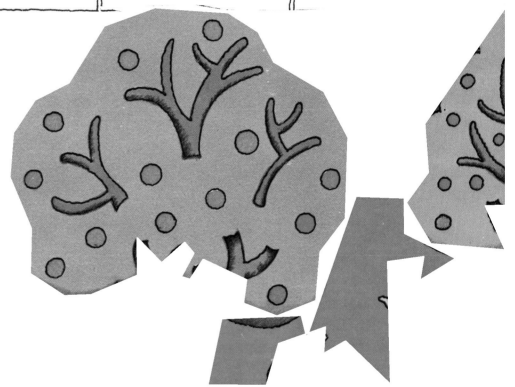

*Why is the highest apple on
a tree always the best one?*
Because it's the tip top apple.

How far can you walk into an apple orchard?
As far as the middle -- after that you are walking out.

What keeps the moon in place?
Its beams.

What is the reddest side of an apple?
The outside.

What does a worm do in a cornfield?
It goes in one ear and out another.

*If your brother has a whole apple
and you only have a bite,
what should you do?*
Scratch it.

Why can't you tell secrets on a farm?
Because the corn has ears, the potatoes have eyes, the beanstalk, and the horses carry tails.

What season is most dangerous?
Fall.

Why did the baby pig eat so much?
To make a hog of himself.

What is it that is too much for one, enough for two,
and means nothing to three?
A secret.

What is a nursery?
A bawl room.

What is never part of anything?
The whole.

Why is a black hen smarter than a white one?
Because a black hen can lay a white egg but a white
hen can't lay a black egg.

What did the doctor say to the patient after the operation?
That will be enough out of you.

What is the difference between a cloud and a kid
being spanked?
One pours rain and the other roars with pain.

What pierces and leaves no hole?
Sound.

Why is an ice cream cone like a race horse?
Because the more you lick it the faster it goes.

Why is the letter A like 12 noon?
Because it's always in the middle of day.

What bird is a thief?
A robin.

What should you do if your toe falls off?
Call a toe truck to take you to the doctor.

How can you tell if elephants have been in your
refrigerator?
By the footprints in the butter.

What question can always be answered "Yes"?
What does Y-e-s spell?

What question can never be answered "Yes"?
Are you asleep?

What is black and white and lives in Puerto Rico?
A lost penguin.

Who is bigger, Mrs. Bigger or her baby?
Her baby is a little Bigger.

Why is it useless to send a telegram to Washington?
Because he's dead.

What do zebras have that no other animals have?
Baby zebras.

Why did the farmer run the steam roller over his fields?
He wanted to raise mashed potatoes.

Why are you like two people when you lose your temper?
Because you are beside yourself.

What letter is never in the alphabet?
The letter in the Post Office.

Why should men stay away from the letter A?
Because it makes men mean.

What did the turkey say before it was roasted?
Boy, am I stuffed.

What prize can a cat win?
The A-cat-emy Award.

Why are statues of George Washington always standing?
Because he could never lie.

Where are elephants found?
They are so big they seldom get lost.

What does a monster do
when he loses a hand?

Goes to a second-hand store.

What do ghosts have for breakfast? Ghost Toasties and evaporated milk.

What do ghosts eat for lunch? Boo loney sandwiches.

What do monsters eat? Things.　**What do monsters drink?** Coke, because Things go better with Coke.

What branch of the Armed Forces did the werewolf join? The Hair Force.

What is a monster's normal eyesight? 20-20-20-20-20.

What should you say when you meet a two-headed monster? Hello. Hello.

Where do monsters get their mail? At the dead letter office.

What do witches put on their hair? Scare spray.

What do you get when you cross a monster with a drip-dry suit? A wash-and-werewolf.

Why don't monsters make good dancers? Because they have three left feet.

How does a monster count to 19? On his fingers.

What is the easiest thing in the world to part with?
A comb.

Why is a snake the most careless animal in the world?
Because he even loses his skin.

What do you do with a blue monster?
Cheer him up.

Why is a cat like the sun?
They both go out at night.

Why won't you starve on the beach?
Because of the sand which is there.

Why are you so tired on April Fools' Day?
Because you have just had a March of 31 days.

What did the polluted water say to the filter?
I hope I make myself clear.

Why do hummingbirds hum?
Because they don't know the words.

How do trains hear?
Through their engineers.

When should you kick about a birthday present?
When you get a football.

What should you do if your dog starts to chew up
the dictionary?
Take the words out of his mouth.

What did Benjamin Franklin say when he discovered
electricity?
Nothing. He was too shocked.

Why do elephants need trunks?
Because they don't have glove compartments.

What is made longer by cutting both ends?
A ditch.

Can you jump higher than a four-foot wall?
Yes. A four-foot wall can't jump.

If you were to throw a white stone into the Black Sea, what would it become?
Wet.

What did one tonsil say to the other?
Get all dressed up. The doctor is taking us out tonight.

What is the highest building in town?
The library. It has the most stories.

Who marries many women but stays single all his life?
A priest.

Which burns longer, a white candle or a black candle?
Neither. Both burn shorter.

Why was the mother flea so upset?
All her children were going to the dogs.

What was the elephant doing on Route 495?
About 3 miles an hour.

A woman had 5 children.
Half of them were boys.
How could that be?

The other half were boys too.

Sixty.

How do you
spell mousetrap
in 3 letters?

CAT.

When life is tough,
what is something you can count on?

Your fingers.

4 mice, 3 dogs, 2 cats
and a kitten went on a picnic.
The kitten said,
"Aren't we 9 having fun?"
Why did the kitten say 9
instead of 10?

The kitten
was too young to count.

Should you say 7 and 9 are 17 or 7 and 9 is 17?
Neither. 7 and 9 are 16.

Five copy cats were sitting on a fence. One jumped off. How many were left?
None. They were all copy cats.

If two is company and three is a crowd, what are four and five?
Nine.

How many 10-cent stamps are there in 2 dozen?
2 dozen.

How many times can 7 be subtracted from 77?
Once. After that it would be subtracted from a smaller number.

What goes 99-clump! 99-clump! 99-clump!?
A centipede with a wooden leg.

How much dirt is there in a hole 1 foot deep, 2 feet wide, and 2 feet long?
none.

How long is a piece of string?
Twice the distance from the middle to the end.

What Roman numeral can climb walls? IV.

55

What did the dentist say to the judge?
I'll pull the tooth, the whole tooth, and nothing
but the tooth.

If you see twenty black cats running down the street,
what time is it?
Nineteen after one.

What did the limestone say to the rock collector?
Don't take me for granite.

Why do carpenters believe there is no such thing as stone?
Because they never saw it.

Why did the goblin quit the game?
Because it didn't have a ghost of a chance.

Why did the baseball team hope the rain kept up?
So that it wouldn't come down.

Why are the tallest people always the laziest?
Because they are longest in bed.

What do they have in Brooklyn that they haven't got
in Manhattan?
The Brooklyn end of the Brooklyn Bridge.

What is the difference between a sewing machine and a kiss?
One sews seams nice and the other seems so nice.

Three children and a Saint Bernard puppy were under
an umbrella but none of them got wet. Why not?
It wasn't raining.

What is quiet when alive and noisy when dead?
A leaf.

What do you get when you cross peanut butter with an elephant?
An elephant that sticks to the roof of your mouth or
peanut butter with a long memory.

Why are all trousers too short?
Because everyone's legs stick out two feet.

If a boy should lose his knee, where can he get another?
At the butcher shop where kid-neys are sold.

What is the best pattern for a banker's suit?
Checks.

How does a witch tell time?
With a witch watch.

What kind of baby should Mr. and Mrs. Sunbeam have?
A very bright one.

What is a skeleton?
Some bones with the people scraped off.

How can you tell the naked truth?
By giving the bare facts.

Why is a crossword puzzle like a fight?
Because one word leads to another.

Who can shave many times a day and still have a beard?
The barber.

Why is an empty pocket always the same?
Because there is no change in it.

Why do ships use knots instead of miles?
To keep the ocean tide.

What did the umbrella say to the scarf?
You go on ahead, I'll cover you.

What always remains down even when it flies up in the air?
A feather.

Why do elephants have such wrinkled knees?
Did you ever try to iron them?

Why is a cloud like Santa Claus?

How much difference is there between the North Pole and the South Pole?

What is the difference between a glass of iced water and a glass of soda?

Why is a goose like an icicle?

What kind of cracker is an icepick?

What is kept in an air-conditioned vault?

How can you tell when there is an elephant in the refrigerator?

What is an eavesdropper?

What do steam engines eat?

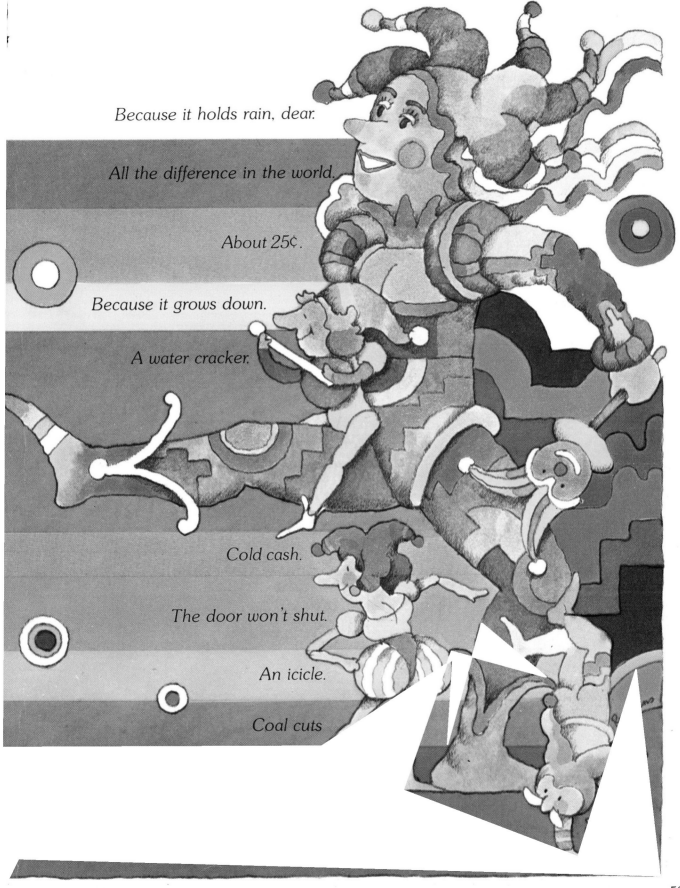

Because it holds rain, dear.

All the difference in the world.

About 25¢.

Because it grows down.

A water cracker.

Cold cash.

The door won't shut.

An icicle.

Coal cuts

Riddles in Code*

What is the opposite of a cool cat? R YFK UFX.

What kind of shoes could you make from banana skins? JCZGGVIJ.

What has two feet and no legs? KNVEKP-WFLI ZETYVJ.

What month has 28 days? KYVP RCC UF.

Who always has guests for dinner? R TREEZSRC.

What did the vampire's son do on the baseball team? YV NRJ KYV SRK SFP.

Have you ever seen a fish cry? EF SLK ZMV JVVE NYRCVJ SCLSSVI.

How do you keep a bull from charging? KRBV RNRP YZJ TIVUZK TRIUJ.

How can you tell when an owl is careless? NYVE YV UFVJEK XZMV R YFFK.

What has everyone seen but will never see again? PVJKVIURP.

What's the best way to grow fat? IRZJV GZXJ.

What does a duck do when he flies upside down? YV HLRTBJ LG.

What do you call an orange that plays the flute? R KFFKP WILZKP.

What is orange, weighs two tons, and has a stick through it?
RE FIREXV YZGGFGFGJZTCV.

What is a supermarket cashier in China? R TYZEVJV TYVTBVI.

How do you fix a short circuit in wiring? CVEXKYVE ZK.

What do you have when a bird flys into your lawn mower?
JYIVUUVU KNVVK.

* See page 62 for help in decoding.

What is the center of gravity? KYV CVKKVI M.

How old would you be if you were very, very fat? KYV JRDV PFL RIV EFN.

To what word can you add a syllable to make it shorter? JYFIK.

What belongs to you but is used more often by others? PFLI ERDV.

What word is always pronounced wrong? NIFEX FW TFLIJV.

How do you talk to a giant? LJV SZX NFIUJ.

What was the largest island before Australia was discovered? RLJKIRCZR.

What did the man step on when it was raining cats and dogs? R GFFUCV.

If sling shots are 50¢, what are window panes? XCRJJ.

What is in the Great Wall of China that the Chinese never put there? TIRTBJ.

What covers itself all summer and goes bare all winter? R KIVV.

What is the best thing to put into pies? PFLI KVVKY.

What has one horn and gives milk? R DZCB KILTB.

What did one potato chip say to the other? CVKJ XF WFI R UZG.

How far can a spook travel? WIFD XYFJK KF XYFJK.

Why did Silly Sammy keep running around his bed?
KF TRKTY LG FE YZJ JCVVG.

What bar opens but never shuts? R TIFNSRI.

What do you call a tailor you have never met? DZJKVI JF REU JF.

Solution to Riddles in Code

The type of code — really a cipher — used for these riddles is called a shift cipher. Every letter of the cipher alphabet stands for a letter in the real alphabet. All the letters are just shifted a *key number* of letters to the right.

To solve the shift cipher for these riddles:

. Write out the real alphabet across the line on a page.

. Put your pencil point on **A** and, starting with **B**, count **9** (the key number) letters.

BCDEFGHIJ

. Write **A** on the line above **J**. (Now you've made the shift.)

. Continue writing out the cipher alphabet over the real alphabet until you reach the real **Z**.

. Go back to the real **A** and continue with the cipher alphabet until you reach the cipher **Z**. Every real letter should have a cipher letter over it.

. Now you have the cipher alphabet. You can solve all the riddles and put anything you want into a secret language. (Do *not* write your homework in cipher.)

. You can make up other shift ciphers just by changing the key number. The key number here is **9,** of course, but try others. Just put your pencil point on **A** and then count over the key number starting with **B.** Put the cipher **A** over the real letter you end on.

Cipher alphabet: R S T U V W X Y Z A B C D E F G H I J K L M N O P Q
Real alphabet: A B C D E F G H I J K L M N O P Q R S T U V W X Y Z
(9 - shift cipher)

Solution example: What is the opposite of a cool cat? Cipher: R YFK UFX.
Solution: A HOT DOG.

Jane Sarnoff graduated from Goucher College and has written two other books for young readers—*A Great Bicycle Book* and *The Chess Book*—which are also illustrated by Reynold Ruffins.

Reynold Ruffins attended Cooper Union in New York City and has won awards from the Society of Illustrators, the Art Directors Club, and the American Institute of Graphic Arts.

Ms. Sarnoff and Mr. Ruffins both live in New York City.

The full-color illustrations for *What? A Riddle Book* are prepared in mixed media, including dyes, acrylics, and sheets of flat transparent color over pencil or ink line. They are camera separated and printed in four colors. The two-color illustrations are pre-separated, prepared as black drawings with brown wash overlays, both reproduced as halftone. All type is Souvenir, set by photo composition.